Praise for Todd 1

Wisdom, more than anything, characterizes his poems. —*Arts & Letters*

As readers encounter the ordinary miracles that Davis reveals as both father and son within "the kingdom of the ditch," they also are reminded that the human is not apart from nature but a part of it. —*Chicago Tribune*

Davis is unflinchingly candid and enduringly compassionate.
—*Harvard Review*

. . . it's time to recognize what an important voice in American poetry we have in Todd Davis. —*Image*

Like poets Wendell Berry and Mary Oliver, Davis is committed and spiritually anchored to his home ground, and so the language rises organically from his daily life. —*Orion*

Through meditations on the flora and fauna of his Pennsylvania home, Davis brings readers into a world rife with danger and darkness as well as quietude and splendor. . . . He reverently observes nature's own poetry and how it illuminates the process of change. —*Publishers Weekly*

As the son of a veterinarian, Davis sees the natural world through a scientist's eyes. Davis knows Latin names, common names, habitats and habits. His poems are steeped in the exactness of the earth and the science that unfolds in wildness, which makes each of his poems a stunning portrait of a time and place. —*Northern Woodlands*

With a sensitivity that could be construed as Audubon-like, Davis takes in the natural world, from its grand glory down to its microscopic necessity. . . . Underlying all these poems are Davis' unyielding connection to and love for nature and the hope that the ills of humanity will be absolved within its eternal fortitude. —*Booklist*

In stunning language and elegant prosody, the poet honors life in its great variety. —*Library Journal*

It's easy to imagine Davis at the top of a swaying Jeffrey pine riding out a storm, Muir-like, all the while jotting down on wet, flapping pages the words he'll later use to describe the energy he feels at the magic of the storm. . . . What a reader will find in Davis's work is a new way to say something old, true, ancient, and familiar. —*Terrain.org*

Davis hunts, fishes, and observes nature in the great tradition of Robert Frost, James Dickey, and Jim Harrison, among others. His poems lead us from the tangible to the intangible and about halfway back again. —*Gray's Sporting Journal*

The poems . . . hold quiet wisdom, not unlike the solemnity and silence of personal prayer. —*Los Angeles Review of Books*

Gratitude and wonder radiate from each of Todd Davis' poems, rendering them sacraments for readers lucky and open-hearted enough to receive them. —*basalt*

Readers familiar with Davis will find his truest gift somehow continues to sharpen. He has that unique ability to link, in a single sentence, the natural world we've become increasingly isolated from to the unnatural world many of us now view as natural. —*Rattle*

COFFIN
HONEY

Books by Todd Davis

POETRY

Native Species

Winterkill

In the Kingdom of the Ditch

Household of Water, Moon, and Snow (limited edition chapbook)

The Least of These

Some Heaven

Ripe

ANTHOLOGIES

Fast Break to Line Break: Poets on the Art of Basketball

Making Poems: Forty Poems with Commentary by the Poets,
    co-edited with Erin Murphy

COFFIN
HONEY

POEMS BY TODD DAVIS

MICHIGAN STATE UNIVERSITY PRESS ▪ *East Lansing*

♾ The paper used in this publication meets the minimum requirements of ANSI/NISO Z39.48-1992 (R 1997) (Permanence of Paper).

 Michigan State University Press
East Lansing, Michigan 48823-5245

LIBRARY OF CONGRESS CATALOGING-IN-PUBLICATION DATA
Names: Davis, Todd F., 1965– author.
Title: Coffin honey / poems by Todd Davis.
Description: First edition. | East Lansing : Michigan State University Press,
    [2022]
Identifiers: LCCN 2021044618 | ISBN 978-1-61186-425-0 (PAPER ; ALK. PAPER) |
    ISBN 978-1-60917-694-5 (PDF) | ISBN 978-1-62895-462-3 (EPUB) |
ISBN 978-1-62896-456-1 (KINDLE)
Subjects: LCGFT: Poetry.
Classification: LCC PS3604.A977 C64 2022 | DDC 811/.6—dc23
LC record available at https://lccn.loc.gov/2021044618

Cover design by Erin Kirk
Cover image *The Bear* by George Boorujy
Dingbat of wild herbs by Ekaterina, Adobe Stock

Visit Michigan State University Press at *www.msupress.org*

For Shelly, Noah & Nathan
—always

will we be / required to view it together / under a gathering sky?

LUCILLE CLIFTON

CONTENTS

COFFIN
HONEY

If We Have to Go

*The pastor / of grief and dreams // guides his flock towards /
the next field // with all his care.*
—DENISE LEVERTOV

When the virus spreads
through the herd,
deer begin to stagger
from drying fields.
They appear in the last
patches of twilight, torn
fur, ribs poking against
the hedges of thinned skin.
The pastor of grief
and dreams waves them
into the road, a suicidal gospel
written on warm macadam.
Blue smoke hovers over us,
every part of the world
on fire. Here in the mountains,
neither grief nor dreams
will save us: what little water
we have our parents use to green
the lawn and frack the ground.
We know we're not part of the flock.
We steal beer from the fridge,
drive the forest road too fast.
At the dam, the reservoir
is an empty eggshell. We peel
tank tops from our sweaty
torsos and sprawl on the concrete
incline, length slanting south,
drinking the afternoon sun.
As if nothing is wrong, mothers

1

call from back porches, pretend
not to notice the empty rooms
we leave behind, while our sisters
practice in mirrors making faces
they think boyfriends will like.
Supper can wait. Along the side
of the highway, dead bodies
of deer bloat, rising like so many
harvest moons. Full of beer,
we play a game: trying to place
a tire over their heads,
bursting the ulcerated boils
to score and finally win.
If we're lucky and hit the mark,
we turn the truck around, point
headlights across the red and pink
smear. The vertical slats of the field
swallow the vanishing light,
and the darkness in our dreams
grows darker.

Buck Day

Downstairs her mom cooks eggs and deer steaks,
pours coffee in the bottom of a cup clouded
with milk and sugar.

Outside her dad talks about a buck on his trail camera,
steam rising from mouth, a reminder of the spirits
that drift up from storm drains in winter.

Her boyfriend works for the township. Like a blood clot
moving through a vein, he walks miles beneath streets
in tunnels of pipe.

She looks forward to these gray days: to sitting quietly
and saying nothing, to absorbing the cold. In the stand,
her shoulder rests against her dad. She lays the rifle, precise
as a ruler, across her lap.

During sophomore year, when she cut herself,
she used a razor in the bathtub. The water blurred red
lines, like a story with no end.

The moon's nearly faded. Her dad nudges her.
Forty yards away a doe and spike figure-eight the field.
He whispers, "Yearlings," says they'll be tender.

On Sunday the minister proclaimed
no one could gaze upon the face of God.
She wonders what the eyes or nose might reveal,
if the burning bush stank like the lamb Adam roasted
on a spit after he was kicked out of the garden.

It's been two years since she stopped cutting.
She rubs Vaseline where the skin knit unevenly,
but pink ridges remain.

She likes the taste of meat but hopes they'll keep running.
Her dad won't let her shoot at a moving deer.

The doe doesn't stop, but the spike falters, halts and bends,
mouth tugging at a fern.

She squeezes the trigger.

On the felt board outside Sunday school, Jesus waits
for Roman soldiers to nail him to the cross.

Her dad smiles as they walk to the animal, says,
"Now the real work," and hands her the knife.

Like field goal posts, the dead buck's legs splay.
She scores the belly and lets the blade run up
the chest, careful not to nick the intestines.

Thomas doubted until he reached his hand into Jesus's side.
With the deer's chest gaping, she touches the trachea
and lungs, imagines the deer opening its mouth to breathe.

It's easy to get lost in the body's house. That's why
she carved openings in her skin.

She cuts away the deer's heart, gives it to her dad,
who slides the warm meat into a plastic bag
where blood, still pooled in one of the chambers,
begins to leak out.

Hunting with Dogs

The mind is made out of the animals
it has attended.
—ROBERT BRINGHURST

All prey is ensouled, and when dogs scent a rabbit or bear's astral body as it lifts and drifts, hot legs strain to carry the rest forward through wet leaves and briars, burs entangled in hair, mud inking pads and pressing a print on naked wood. They stand on hind legs and bark at the treed being, spirit having caught up and joined flesh: desire satisfied as they rend it from bone to taste the sweet marrow of consciousness oozing from an eye socket. The oldest dog has hunted with the man for nearly a decade, part of him like an arm or leg, like the rifle his father handed him when he turned eight. Thirty-five thousand years ago, the first pup was snatched from a den-litter, and the she-wolf snarled, howl-screamed her hatred from the lid of a small cave: pup carried by the nape to a village where the hunter chewed bison fat, viscous-gray meal the small wolf licked and learned to love, lapping at scraps, a bone saved from the stewpot. Driving hounds up the mountain, the man doesn't know the full history of why his dogs can hold an animal, pin it in a tree, or corner it where stone sheers to wall. We've grazed the earth for such a long time, canine teeth swerving cheek, holy kiss from a mouth formed for blood. The first drawn breath suggests all animals share one soul, and because hound and man have breathed together over the ragged bodies they've chased, because in deep snow or rocky field they've dragged the dead to feed the living, their souls are snared in the same sprung trap. After the hunter guts the prey, lays intestines to air, lungs to sun, the dogs lust-lick with a sense of justice. A command must always have a reward.

Music for Film before the Destruction of a Drone

Guarding this / / frontier, we double silence, wander /
narrow passes where clouds are born.
—WEI YING-WU

The drone dips overhead, tiny camera-eye
peering down, a diminished god who still longs
for intimacy. In a desert bunker more than 2000
miles away, a man receives live footage of the top
of Ursus's enormous skull where memory's
incessant appetite craves the comfort
of his dead mother's breasts. The man who sees
only what the camera sees drinks coffee, drizzles
artificial creamer into a Styrofoam cup,
and loses his way in the dissolving white powder.
As if to shrug away a pest, Ursus rolls his shoulders,
stops to gape at the mechanical bee
that pollinates a far flower of rectangular screens.
He doesn't understand what it means
to be pixelated, dissected into smaller
and smaller squares. Who might wish to stare
as he squats to defecate or couples with another,
stumbling away in a postcoital haze? The man
who toggles the drone perceives a muffled aura,
tries to adjust the display. He thinks better of telling
his supervisor and instead watches what looks like
coltsfoot duff ruffled in wind. Ursus tries to name
what descends: an awkward raven or crow that struggles
through branches. Whatever this flying thing is,
it emits a metallic buzzing that sends grackles winging
for cover. When Ursus's mother died, he waited
with the body, ear pressed to the center of her chest,
wrinkled nipple like the soul's eye. He longed for
the portion that must leave, and from the blackest part
a shape rose and walked among gnarled trunks, an assurance

6

the stories she told were true. What's the appropriate
music for extinction? A fugue, because death
must be allowed to sing? An oratorio, because we all play
a role in what vanishes? A nocturne? We'd do well
to remember extirpation can include light, too.
The man notes the pads and nails of Ursus's paws,
bear-gesture like an overture, furred arms orchestrating
the drone's demise. If the screen hadn't gone blank,
the man would have witnessed the unquiet ghost
of Ursus's mother breathing in her son's body,
bringing the flightless wings to mouth, plastic
cutting gums, a fragment lodging in a hole
where long ago researchers pried out a premolar
trying to determine his age. Sunlight catches
on shiny metal, and a crescendo of grackles
flutters up from an orchestra pit
of tupelo leaves. The iridescent blue
of their heads tips back so they can be heard
croaking and squeaking, high-pitched whistles
opening like a rusty gate, the closest these birds
will ever come to singing.

Taxidermy: Cathartes aura

When the vulture fell
from the sky, the boy gathered
the outstretched wings and folded
the body to his breast, feathers
cresting his shoulder, a span
of plumage for riding thermals,
drifting ever higher
above the earth.

The bird's spiraling descent
was unexpected like when
his uncle touched him
in the cellar as he shoveled
coal for winter, telling him
he couldn't have the fried
doughnuts sprinkled
with confectioner's sugar
if he screamed
or told his mother.

Over the next week
the boy slit the dead bird
from neck to tail feathers,
pulled out what had grown inside,
and used cornstarch to dry
the wet residue. He wished to keep
some semblance of the bird
alive before the memory
migrated and was forgotten.

His uncle's white whiskers
stung his cheeks, coffee-breath
at his ear demanding he remove
his pants and later wash
the blood-soaked underwear
at the sink in the garage.

While he worked, tears fell
into the dark space
he'd opened to insert
wires beneath the wings,
around the fragile ribs.
It hurt to sit and burned
when he bore down, excrement
swirled red in the toilet.

In the days that followed
his uncle wanted more,
but the boy begged,
and the man made him take it
in the mouth instead.

He woke with decay in his nostrils
and tried to figure the nature
of the bird's death, but found no bullet
or pebbled buckshot, no evidence
to explain any of this.

He assumed it would go on
until he was older, big enough
to drive a fist into his uncle's throat,
or for that man to keel over,
heart given out while skinning
a raccoon he'd trapped
or turning sod in the garden.

The boy believed the bird
had become the thing
it coveted, having consumed
so much dead flesh, and he stuffed
the cavity with rags and cotton,
sewed the incision and dangled it
with fishing-line over his bed.

Each night before he closed his eyes,
he stared at the pink head, the only
resurrection he believed in now,
and when his mother extinguished
the hall light, he prayed
to the shadow that hung above
to show him how to take flight.

Rooster

The boy clutches the rooster, claws extended toward dirt.
The boy's hair is shorn to the scalp and he wears no shirt.

The rooster's comb stands straight up.
Hens scratch gravel and stink of sour crop.

Because they need extra money, his mother lets people dump
cars in the field. The junkyard smells of dead rats the cats kill.

Veins map the boy's skull bright blue in the sun.
His mother tells him this is their family-tree written down.

The rooster sounds a signal, and like an old man's testicles,
the red folds beneath the beak quiver.

The boy's toy-spurs scuff the wood on the porch.
Fighter jets from the military base rattle the glass.

When his mother's in bed with the neighbor, the boy watches
TV and follows the grooves on his head with his fingers.

Every four weeks his mother traces the rivers with clippers,
reciting names from a different branch of the family.

At school a sixth-grader shows the boy a cockfight
on his phone. He's not allowed to say *cock* at home.

After school he goes to the barn to find the bird
and pushes his finger against its spur.

The boy doesn't know how he knows
the names before his mother speaks them.

Today, on the rooster's back, he writes in bloody letters
the words *Stonewall* and *Jackson*, then repeats them.

What I Know about the Last Lynching in Jeff Davis County

How it happened more than fifty years before I was born. How nobody in our family talks about it. How I learned in history class that white people strung up black people. How my cousin Mary Lou has dark skin because my uncle's brown as hemlock bark. How some still don't take kindly to my mom's sister marrying the way she did. How Mary Lou and me listen for the sound of water on the mountain and follow it under rhododendron. How our history teacher was suspended by the school board for saying blacks still get lynched when police choke them. How we catch and split speckled trout. How my uncle taught us this. How when we go to Dollar General for worms, a clerk trails Mary Lou up and down each row while I steal gum and two jawbreakers. How the orange wound of the fish's skin reveals the sweet pink we fry in butter and salt. How the dad of our best friend has a confederate flag on his truck's back window. How when we suck on the jawbreakers, our tongues and teeth turn blue and red. How my uncle won't go into the bar on Main Street. How some say that black man had to die on the tree because he whistled at a white woman. How me and Mary Lou made a book about it. How my uncle still says *Yes sir* to every white man he speaks to. How Mary Lou can draw near anything. How once she made a picture of a black and white warbler that's taped to the back of my bedroom door. How we never showed anyone that book. How I wrote the story so the man could come back to life like Jesus. How my uncle taught us to whistle like that bird. How we buried the book in a tin box in the woods. How we still use that whistle to warn if someone's coming. How I worry about my uncle when I think of our best friend's dad. How Mary Lou drew other black men cutting the man down from the tree. How the tree understood the man would miss the soft skin on the back of his daughter's arms. How Mary Lou says the bird is striped like prison bars. How the oak is rotting from a fungus now. How the branches keep breaking off.

For Ross Gay

Bad Seed

Before her boyfriend leaves for Fort Bragg,
she lays with him between gnarled
trunks in the tall grass. The orchard's
hair is tangled, the fruit small and sour.
The family that labored this hollow
fled forty years before. No one visits
to pick anymore. The clouds move fast,
and she feels a pinprick, like fire
as thumb and forefinger pinch candle.
Looking up, she sees the indented
foreheads of apples, sunken cheeks,
the chins cleft at odd angles.

As the Mountain Grows Dark

Plastic tubes worm from Granny's nose. A shiny tank holds
oxygen to replace the heavy air in these mountains

where coal is dug and burned in stoves. From the other room,
voices on a talk show yell out who they think the baby's father is.

The girl rubs her belly and wonders how long before she shows.
If Granny knew, she'd tell her granddaughter to get on her knees

and pray, to ask God to take the sin and make something good.
In the kitchen, blue-veined hands strip rattlesnake meat,

dipped in buttermilk and egg, coated in cornmeal and pepper
and laid in bubbling bacon-grease. When the greens are well on,

and the cornbread nearly done, the old woman shuts off the oxygen,
lifts a half-smoked cigarette between yellowed teeth.

The girl hasn't seen the boy since he left for training
and then a tour in Iraq. He didn't even suspect. The girl's father

hunts rattlers high on the mountain where males slither to mate
in July and August, secreted in cribs of stone. He waits for them

to be done, wants more snakes in the coming years. But after:
he rakes them with a hook, machetes the neck, and collects

the rattles to nail on a board in the shed. A coughing fit shakes
Granny. She sips Robitussin until the quaking subsides.

The girl hears of a clinic over the state line but can't imagine
stopping what grows inside. Rattlesnakes don't lay their eggs.

They carry them deep within, to ward off a crack or the hungry
glance of a raccoon or fox. When the three sit down

to eat off TV trays in the front room, it's all smiles, light
from a rerun flickering. Snakes bear their brood on rocky ground,

allow their young to stalk after they've shed a first skin.
The girl unbuttons the top of her jeans, feels something like a kick.

Her fingers and lips shine, snake white and glistening.
A locust-song flares while a buzzing takes up in the air.

The mountain grows dark for the night.

Before the Miscarriage

Still early, still naked,
only a green haze
of leaves before
spring's first shade.

An unfettered sun
shows her a lady
slipper, pink flower
that looks like a small
girl's shoe or a baby's
furled lung.

Her granny taught her
not to pick or dig it up.
Taken from its place,
it withers and dies.

Churching the Cow

When the cows are calving, we pasture the donkeys
to comfort them. Momma says they're like the garlic
and marigolds that keep rabbits away from the garden.
The dogs who pack together in the swamp will tear
a newborn to jigsaws, wolf down the pieces, and leave
stomachs to puzzle placenta. Killing the young is the oldest sin.
When the donkeys catch a feral motion, they bray a signal,
ring the group and rise up with stone hooves.

A single kick can rend a skull. I've seen brains bleed out.
Cow licking afterbirth and canine blood, then presenting
a pink nipple to a searching mouth. As soon as the young
are delivered, Momma ties a rag to the cow's tail
and lights a candle. Together we pass the flame over back
and under belly, making a circle three times as a blessing.
In the morning we shovel the dead into a wheelbarrow
and haul the remains to the pigsty.

Ursus in the Underworld

For everything that rises must converge.
—PIERRE TEILHARD DE CHARDIN

Plott hounds scramble the tunnel's rock, yowling
and scenting Ursus's shadow. They're devoured
by the dark the deeper they go. Their masters
who have trained them won't descend, having chased
the bear the better part of the day. They build a fire
at the entrance to wait and consider the small extinctions
of the self, outlined in a string of tobacco spit.
Running downward beneath the earth's ceiling
exposes the frailty of light, and in the underworld,
where dreams reside, Ursus finds evidence
that bear have lived since before the foundation
of the world: Callisto searing the sky with Ursus's name,
her child Arcas joining her. Everything that rises
must converge, but over a lifetime hounds will fight
and rifles bark fire that blisters bone. For years the skeleton
of Ursus's mother lay uncovered on a talus slope
where during a summer storm she was struck by lightning.
The flame transformed bits of memory into a bone-pyre.
Beneath the moon and stars, the beacon burned like a dog's
beautiful baying. Now the ridge above Monture is mostly ash,
and deep in its sooty stomach, where the dogs corner Ursus,
the transmitters that ring the Plotts' necks fail, leaving silence
in the empty hands of the waiting hunters. Hades wore the head
of a bear as he chased Persephone: lust being the work we do
in death as in life. Out of this underworld the green
luminescence of the first dog's eyes is birthed, wisest
of hounds who recognizes the bear as the messenger of death.
It climbs out of the blackness, captured in a flashlight's halo,
head poking from one of the crudely dug air vents,
covered in coal dust and blood, ear torn
where Ursus tried to whisper his secret.

dream elevator

a boy

        whose uncle touched him in the cellar

descends

        the shaft of sleep

into coal-burning darkness

                the mine reeks

        of methane and urine

anthracite

      scabs

     veins emptied

no place left

         to stick a needle

a tunnel

        into vanishing

     mountains

shaken

      folded

with past sins

         he clambers

through a hole

                    into a cavern

ceiling echoed

                    with light

from a headlamp

          a bottomless

                    underground lake

that collects the bodies

of the dead

                  coal cars

overturned

              floating belly up

like blind fish

        rusting

              pickaxe

                        tanning

        the current

while

              somewhere above

                  his mother lies

in a tub

water tepid
                    skin sluffing

                              scales

like deceit

          the secret

knowledge

                    of her child's

violation

          a heat
                    that fogged the mirror

gone

          now
                              the memory

          of a baby

                    crawling over linoleum

lost

          as well

          where the river surfaces

and

a drowned

            cousin

            who tries

      to climb

                  the mountain

from the inside

            wedged

                into

a crevice

                where

          a boy holds

a pail

      of newts

collected at the seep

                following

the bear

      that he tells

no one

         about

fetid

scat

     in cane breaks

day old

  fawn

  ripped open

like an envelope

    so

    the boy

  must replace

logs and rocks

   tossed for grubs

must rake the trail

    with branches

  to cover

their passage

    clay-caked

claws scraping

    on

  the elevator panel

                        steel box

rising
                        on metal

            cords

                        carrying

mined
                        grief

a boy's and his mother's

shared

                lifted

from darkness

                        like a mouth

to a roughened nipple

                        a half-waking

body
                washed

                by fern and sorrel

wildness

                leached

                        not the taste

but the warmth

        pearls of milk

on tongue

the sound
            of another

suckling

(cub
      or
           human)

no difference

        when a mother

decides

      to take

her life

Mother

After the animal that drank sound died, the world
lay still and cold for months.
—WILLIAM STAFFORD

She drank sorrow, bringing my face
to her neck. She drank the kingfisher's
clicking, pileated's knocking. She drank
the clatter the creek makes when it rains.
She drank frost heaves, widowmakers
descending in wind. She chewed leafduff
scratched away by the flowering of polygala
and violet. She lapped at the dark
cries of coyote and barred owl, rabbit
bleats devoured. Before wings disappeared,
she opened her mouth to the erratic
flight of bats. When I fell from the tree,
she drank the wound on my back, spooned
the sound of a rat snake eating mice
beneath the porch. She loved cricket chirp,
the metal of cicada scritch-scritching.
She swallowed the stomp of mules, the snarl
of dogs. She said the red moon, rocketing
the sky, was like kerosene on kindling,
a fire to illuminate our insides. I asked how
a river buries itself when it dies.
She laughed and drank the weariness
of such questions. I need to be more
careful, to listen intently and learn
to drink better. It's been months
since I conjured her voice.

What Her Father Taught Her

After two years with little rain the river shrank. I didn't think
water could go so quick from fat to thin. The deep hole
under the trestle stayed deep, but when we jumped
it took longer to get there. Each day in August, as the heat
started to fade, we'd walk the rail line to the bridge
and let our legs dangle over the gulch the earth had whittled.
Winds would come up, catch the cold left in the river and remind
us of betrayal. No trains for the past ten years, but Mom

likes to tell how Dad worked for Norfolk Southern. She won't say
a word about the woman who shot him. Before he died
he taught me how ginseng's fruit tumbles from its stalk,
how those red seeds in September need to be cast
in a furrow after harvesting the root. When I fall
through the air, just before I hit the water, I like to think
I'm no different than a seed entering the earth
or a bullet sliding into the darkness of a chamber.

Coffin Honey

I.

Bees dying.

In hive.

Beneath petals.

Among engineered

leaves and blades,

the zippered pods

of glistening beans.

A chemical sun

showering kernelled light.

II.

The beekeeper raises a bee-box lid,

    scrapes bodies

from comb, wax filling

    behind fingernails,

embalmed

    in stickiness.

III.

Honey made by the dead
is sweet.

The dead floating in honey
makes a daughter weep.

IV.

Fingers to lips.

        Fingers to tongue.

                Tongue crossing teeth.

                        A boat ferrying the dead.

                                Traversing the river

                                        of our mouths.

V.

Fingerprints:

      whirls

of deceit

left

on whatever

      we

beseech.

VI.

The beekeeper's daughter searches for survivors.
Surveys the forest canopy for remaining swarms
to gather and take back to her father.

At the end of a branch, she finds striped bodies
crawling over one another, swaying in air, a sound
like her mother's as the tumor consumed her.

VII.

The first time she's stung

                           she jumps,

screams,

                  runs out

into a clover-drenched

                              field

where she thinks

                she's safe.

VIII.

A face made of bees

       flies to the edge

of the woods, hovers

       there, turns and shakes

its head

       in disapproval.

IX.

As lungs fill,
she hears
a buzzing inside
her.

As if she's
a bee flying
to the center
of the hive.

X.

The beekeeper

  finds

the body

  in tall grass,

green and shaking

  with wind:

  puffed

with welts,

  purpled

from loss

  of oxygen,

cankered

red

  from the shock

of trying

  to help.

XI.

In the cool of the cellar,
in the dim light

just beneath the lip
of the earth,

he builds a small box,
five feet by three, milled

less than a month before
from a beetle-infested pine.

XII.

The beekeeper smothers
                    the girl

          in streams
                    of honey,

                    only her front

teeth
          showing,
                    the same

as when she suckled

                    her mother,
                    and after

her mother's
          death,

                    her thumb.

XIII.

The stink of earth
                    opened.

XIV.

Scratch of shovel
        and pick.

Repetition of ruin.

Hands keeping time
        with the clang.

XV.

Late at night, drunk on mead,
the beekeeper recites the story
of a body fed only honey:

How the girl who ate
amber for each meal
smelled of clover

and goldenrod,

how she shined

like a thousand sunflowers

looking directly

into the sun.

Dowser

He liked to say the water in us seeks the water
beneath the ground: rivers that begin as seeps
high up in the mountains and disappear
beneath the membrane of limestone valleys,
eating the bedrock to form caves and underground
lakes where a sea used to be. He claimed
a cousin saw the skeleton of a whale
surface in the middle of a Nebraska field,
stalks of wheat like krill sifted
through the fossil record. We wrote to him
because we needed a well: the walk
to the river too far, our pails too small.
He came three days to hold his willow-fork
like a plow, to plod forward with eyes rolled
toward heaven. He stumbled through tall grass,
past a grove of cedars, then strode to a flat place
where his arms began to shake, his lips to hiss.
At that spot the men stabbed the sod
with shovels, and we stood, witnesses to what God
set swimming there.

Field Sermon

Men are not where he is / Exactly now, but they are around
him / around him like the strength / Of fields.
—JAMES DICKEY

Walking the mile through blossoming laurel to church,
the preacher wallows clay banks along the river, wailing

a song with furrows. He wants to remember this place
when he stands at the altar, slicked red, barefoot tracks

across the pine floor. He'll chastise what's left
of the congregation for not having faith that corn

will sprout, pole beans plump and wrapped around the legs
of a trellis. Vultures circle a month with no rain,

and a voice swings from the belly, like the stump chains
he uses to drag trees from the woodlot. Raphael and Azrael,

the mules he named after reading the Book of Revelation,
bear the weight, and slowly the field reveals itself in unfolding

absence. As if they were in the presence of an archangel,
trees buckle and kneel, and he hauls them on a skid of words:

salvation, repentance, sin, a backward formula he believes in.
Like a tick at the edge of a dog's ear, his face bloats

when he shouts *grace*, a puzzle as convoluted as wild carrot's
lace, dangerous as hogweed's sap. He loves the story of the man

blinded by it, struck down like Paul near Damascus, arcing
a scythe to the base of the stalk, umbrella of flowers

causing boils to rise from his arms and scales to scar his eyes.
He believes God asks us to suffer as Christ suffered, thorns

biting the skull, sin's venom veining its way to the heart.
When he castrates the hogs in spring, he hollers a line

from Leviticus, knowing how he loves the pink fat,
thanking Jesus he can fry it in a pan without retribution.

When his voice grows raspy, a rusted hinge in need of mercy,
he holds out his hands like a tin cup to where the seep streams

from a cleft in the rock. Thirst slaked, a piece of jerky hangs
like a rat's tail from the corner of his mouth. This past fall

he set aside two ewes, choosing not to breed them.
The ram horn-smashed every fence and gate, a victim

of interrupted lust. The preacher culled the beast, slaughtered
and ground into sausage. He knows even the beloved

will be tempted, and temptation is an empty corncrib,
milking cow butchered for meat, children left with no milk

to drink. All around him hushed *Amens* echo from hemlock limbs,
the fevered *Hallelujahs* of a poplar careen like a logging truck

near a bend. He lifts his arms to the sky and asks the newly
cleared field, *Brother, who is your true lover? Sister,*

in whose bed do you lie at night? As if in answer, he hears rattles
before he sees the den of snakes gathered in the root-space

left by a beech. This ball of serpents tangles with what he's
convinced are the demands of faith. God is with him,

or the morning cool enough to have dulled the rattlers,
so when he picks one it doesn't strike, allows him to stroke

its ridged skin, to drape it like a preaching scarf around his neck.
Seduction of coils caressing the throat as he whispers a prayer

and kneels in sunlit soil. The fang's sting isn't so different
from what he feels when he tends his bees, but shock slithers out

like a snake's tongue, slurs his speech, as if he's been taken
by the Spirit: a babble over turned earth.

Lambing

But when you do a charitable deed, do not let your left hand
know what your right hand is doing . . .
—MATTHEW 6:3

On her knees, the woman nuzzles the lamb to her breast,
guides new mouth to ewe's nipple, lays down in hay
with mother and child. She wakes at 2 a.m.,
mountain-cold seeping like water into a boulder's
fissure. In the warmth of her own room, she dreams
of the first wet-flash, streams of blood at the opening.
Unlike the others, this one falters, stumbles sideways
and collapses. At the first hint of light she meets the ewe
at the gate, animal longing for pasture. Her children

are still in bed but will need breakfast in another hour.
She finds the abandoned lamb in a corner and bends
to pick him up, to carry him to the hemlock near the hilltop.
She follows the faint groove of a centuries-old logging road,
knife's weight in front pocket. Pushing against thigh,
the sheep-child's head lolls, no strength to hold its weight.
Her left hand strokes the brow and neck, lifts jaw
toward purpled sky, while her right hand brings the stone-
sharpened knife across the throat.

For Melanie Viets

Tattoos Cataract Her Back

Her brother draws each with needle-fire.
A register of what their parents
and grandparents took without asking.
Waterfall of birds that flew into the cyclone
of history: pagan reed-warbler, least
vermilion flycatcher, Laysan honeycreeper,
and Marianne white-eye.

When she walks to the store, children grab
her hands, small fingers spiderwalking
the raw leaves of feathers that decorate
her flesh. At the base of her spine a nest.
Three eggs—one red, one blue, one yellow.
Inky cracks that trickle their sides.
A cowbird flies just above, waiting to pilot
its own egg into this grassy oval. She wishes
they were safe in her womb: sky devoid
of planes and drones, the metal windmills
that knock avian bodies to the ground.

Audubon shot the birds he painted.
Vast rafters beneath the roof of trees.
Calls so loud, even shouting to his companion,
hands cupped around lips, he couldn't be heard.

To conceal this secret, she sews long dresses,
shrouds these lives deep in the silent woods
of her thighs where Carolina parakeets
grasp branches. The lowest stares
straight ahead, as if it can see its own demise:
yellow head with a face like butternut squash;
green wing-feathers spread to reveal lines
that melt in vertical streaks.

Her husband's hands glide up her legs,
and he delights in the calls that spring
from her pursed lips. Something close
to what the parakeet might have cried
as it mated.

Bog Parable

Entering these deep woods, late sunlight
flares on green moss again, and rises.
—WANG WEI

Ursus steps onto moss: buoyancy of time

    recorded in layers of sphagnum, trapped water

and larch light, the early October red of cranberry.

    He's heard the baying of dogs who hunt him.

(Bear are born understanding the eternal.)

    Yet the floating world remains below. Distant

in the forest a gunshot and the gutting of an animal

    who joins eternity. Today, after many days

without a single dragonfly, a blue-eyed darner

    bobs the air, whirls around Ursus's head,

and with wings of wax, flies toward the sun.

dream elevator

In time

               like mold in a washbasin

the plague

         which we made

         which we are

    grew

        (warmth and water)

    lungs provide both

in ample measure

                  tents of bodies

                       collapsing

        as in a windstorm

leg-poles bent

        flaps of skin torn

               death always

    flies

quickly

       a thousand crows

              a puzzle

of sky

         thin cracks of light

    a map

         that shows the way

to suffering.

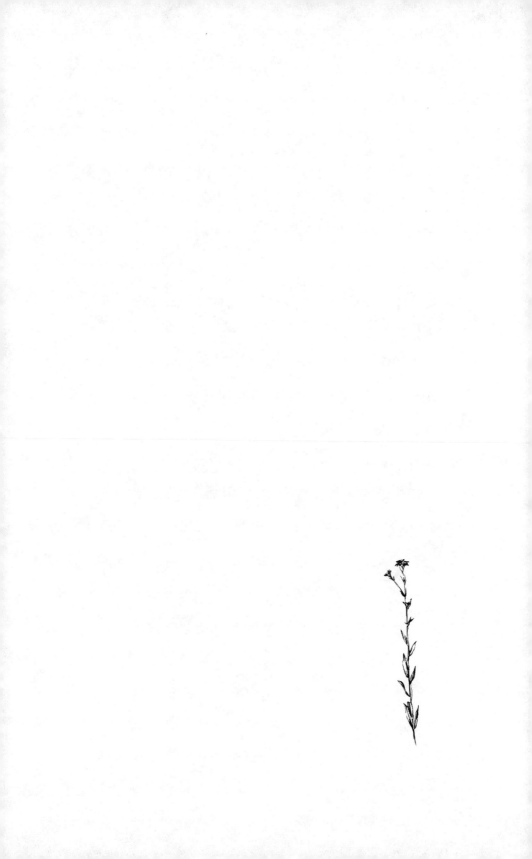

Extinction

Children gather at the water to search for the dead, each
with a lantern sending a spear of light over the waves.
They've been taught, when they find themselves
wading too far out, to follow the shapes of crows and ravens
until they reach the sandy bank. There the birds write
in white excrement about what we've done. This isn't an apologue,
no moral to be spoken by a dying bear, by a turkey, tail fanned
in wisdom, beard grown long with irony. Some of the children
have begun to dream the same dream: arms transformed to paper
wings, a strong wind tearing holes. In the dead snags that rise
from the marsh, twelve vultures perch, confirming that pallbearers
are always the last to die. Each night before the children light
their lanterns and walk into the dark, they read from a book
that begins, *Dear Prophecy, please don't come true.*
But death's contagious. The musical avarice of maggot
and carrion beetle attractive. Look how clean the bones are,
how they've been put to rest carefully. If you lay the femur
and humerus end-to-end, the outline of a lost continent emerges.
We drew the map we're consigned to wander. Some of us pretend
we'll go on living.

Possum

In deep summer, when the creek dries up,
copperheads stir like water on limestone, ripples
that steal a gaze and stay you in place. The crossbands
on their backs, like hourglasses, run down to death.
Daddy carries a .22, shoots near anything that moves.
When he was a child, a sister lost part of an arm to venom.
Gangrene crawling like a colicky baby toward her breast.
Bone saw was the only thing to arrest it. Mamaw claims
a nick in the moon ushers in mating, musk like cucumbers
in the garden. I found my snake-killer riding the back
of his dead mother in the red gravel along the road.
Nose like a pink flower sticking up through matted fur.
I don't know what happened to his brothers. Didn't check
the pouch. It was no secret what the tire did. I picked him up
like a sack of millet. He bared his teeth. Tiny opposable
thumbs clamped to my fuck-you finger. Don't kill a possum.
They'll murder copperheads for you. Clear snakes
from stonewalls. Usher the dead from under squash
and pumpkin leaves. You should see him sit up
and take notice when I dangle a gizzard over his craw.
You'd swear a smile wrinkles that sour face.

Up on Blue Knob

most of the men possess one leg
shorter than the other, femur whittled
by thousands of hours wrestling
a plow along ridgeline. Because the mules
the men follow are fashioned by the hollow's
pitch as well, the farrier trims hooves at an angle,
builds shoes to compensate. Wives and mothers,
when they call on kin in the valley, limp
across flat ground, hips unused to anything
but the swell and fall of the mountain.
For ten years children run with a normal gait,
the length it takes gangly limbs to sprout,
to learn to balance the sole inheritance
granted by this slanted world.

Foot Washing

She flinches when he caresses her foot, rubs thumb
over ridged callus grown like a furrow through a summer
of no shoes. Weeds hoed, corn and beans picked.
Each year her mother buys one pair of shoes to last
the frozen ground from November to April. The last two
she outgrew before the first violet. With a butcher knife,
her father cut away the toe-box so she wouldn't blister.
The minister tells her to think on the savior pouring water
from a pitcher, dust clouding the basin with a muddy plume.
We must shed the world, he says. The girl wonders why
you'd want to be rid of the only home you have.
In the pink of May, with feet bared, she loves the earliest
strawberries, groan of bullfrogs, the pulsing, high pitched
call of spring peepers when the ice goes out of the pond,
which sounds like a hundred young chickens frightened by a fox.
This man her parents trust recites the story of the woman
who washed Christ's feet with tears, anointed them with nard,
and dried them with her long black hair. This morning
on the way to church, at the river's edge, she rubbed sand
over soles, trying to erase the stains of fieldwork, afraid
of the strong smell of sweat, the manure she shuttles
from the stalls in the barn. And now she shakes as he wipes
the top of her foot, his fingers brushing her ankle bone.
Nobody but her mother has ever touched her feet.

Blind Horse

The farmer's children
lead the horse
who sees
nothing but darkness
by the halter
into the farthest
pasture where
the clover smells
pink over everything
and a small stream
splashes blue
against its banks,
the sound reminding
the horse of brown
furrows the plow dug
years ago
as he strained
against the will
of the farmer
and the stubborn
stone-filled soil, red-
winged blackbirds
whistling from cedar
posts where the farmer
stretched barbed
wire silvery tight
and caught the belly
hair of deer
as they leapt
into the neighbor's
field, a distant
memory for this horse
who now lives

mostly in memory,
a place like lumpy
sod after it's turned:
black, and then
more black, as far as
the eye can see.

The Book of Miracles

Despite Ursus's approach
the fawn remains curled, delicate
calligraphy attempting to mimic
crinkleroot and leafduff.

Like a held breath, the disguise
falters, and the stream's clapping
masks the bear's shuffled gait.

With three nails, Ursus opens
the book of miracles and reads
the fawn's newly written muscle:
ink the color of ginseng berries,
taste like copper wounded with salt.

The book of miracles, when recited,
sounds like tendon and cartilage
cracked, snap of shoulder moving
out of joint, slurp of marrow.

Before any of this, the heart,
sweetest and most joyous of meat,
is purchased by the mouth
with singing groans.

Such holy books aren't new.
Ursus himself was resurrected
by the light that grows each day,
that causes everything to climb
upon the back of another
and eat until full.

What's left of the fawn
doesn't squirm in his belly,
but as Ursus sleeps, the doe-mother
forages where she left her child:
nipples aching, rivulets of milk
running down slender legs.

Foxfire

In the valley, where corn and beans grow in rows
mapped by GPS, farmers feed cows and hogs tetracycline

and testosterone. After butchering them in dark tin buildings,
they slop the remains to the survivors so the animals, shoulder-

to-shoulder, eat their own kind. At night, because of the lights
the townspeople burn on their porches or hang from posts

to comfort themselves, only the brightest stars are woven
into the black. The heat of summer lasts too long,

and the boy who lives on the mountain is raised from the sweat
of his bed to look down on the town's spectral glow.

He can't hear the corn-leaves rustle when the breeze
from the poisoned river swells, but he smells the paper mill

and thinks about swimming in what pours from its pipes,
the carp he fishes for that turn on their sides.

Where a fire scorched the dirt the year he was born
huckleberries grow on a talus slope near the peak.

To escape the heat, he climbs to the field in the dark and stands
on the biggest rock, stretching arms like an egret.

Flight's a kind of forgiveness, and here fireflies blink
mercifully among berry branches, miniature lamplighters

finishing their rounds for the night. They rise up and drift
about his head, landing on arms and legs, gloving fingers

in a green luminescence. As if he were a rotting log in a swamp,
laced with fungus that pulses like a star, he joins the milk-wash

of the infinite, a beacon for other heavenly bodies
already falling in bright streaks to the earth.

Snapper

In May, even in rain, she walks the river
searching for orphaned goslings, ducklings
cast off. Her brother laughs when he steers
the canoe, separating a small bird from a gaggle.
She looks back and out of the wake an open
mouth. Smear on the surface the only sign
of theft. Over supper her mother swears
the gosling felt nothing. The girl knows better
than anyone the gravel banks where the turtles
bury their eggs. She carries an awl she stole
from her father's workbench. For every
duck or goose they take, she pierces the side
of a shell, turns it over so the yolk oozes out.

Relics

Farm work steals bones. Johnny's ring finger lost
to a cultivator. Aunt Susan's big toe to a potato
planter. Last fall a combine gobbled Grandpa Harry's leg
from the knee down. Everyone in the family insists
the bones are ours. Nurses fuss and refuse at first,
until we threaten a lawyer. We bring them all home.
Stored in a cedar chest, lined with a red wool blanket.
We organize the skeletons by date, by the cost of the work
we were doing before each accident. Building a barn's
worth more than tossing hay bales. Drilling a well's a prize
compared to moving an outhouse, even if the privy's full.
The day Mom was kicked in the head milking Mildred—
a cantankerous Guernsey we should've shot for pot roast—
her eyes rolled back, flashing like fish just beneath the surface
of consciousness. Her brain swelled, and they cut a hole
in the skull to relieve the pressure. I imagined the deep lake
of her cortex. How I'd drop a line in the augered circle,
like ice-fishing, trying to catch something golden
to mount and put in a case. Another relic to pray to,
so we could be blessed by what's taken from us.

dream elevator

Cities burning.

An ash-filled river.

A few humans

like vessels washed in milk

pole boats

through the river's sludge,

careful not to touch

the water.

A woman who fed us

reduced to salt and tar.

My mother

held me to the ground,

body like a roof.

She whispered an elegy

to her fur

as it burned.

I saw the pink of dusk

on the ground

as she sheltered me.

No screens.

No buildings.

No cars.

Static left the air.

As we once did

we do so again

scratching images

on the bark of trees.

Bear-Eater

Now there are bear dreams again for the bear-eater.
—JIM HARRISON

After I ate the warm heart of the bear, I slept,
and when I woke, a bobcat eyed my lips, my red fingers
gripping the emptied purse.

A hunger flutters the skull like a swallowtail bumping
against the boned dome of sky.

The oldest bears, with milky eyes, see through water clearly.

How easy to catch speckled trout when you follow fins
between rock folds.

Ten thousand shades of green crowd the understory
while the long history of earth's turning comes to rest
in a bog where white pine stumps rot
like the sawed-off legs of mastodons.

The ancients named the rivers we haven't found yet.

We hide beneath licked limestone, flow for miles
underground.

I worry about when the next cubs will be born.
How we might go on, you and I, this species
we've become.

To clear my head I drink from a small spring,
settle into a patch of sunlight emptied
by dead ash trees.

We mustn't forget to listen
for the faint singing
that drifts up through the cracks
in the streambed.

High in a snag, raven plays priest, croaks
a line about death from the scriptures
written on the creases of corvid brains.

Just now I don't want another death song.

I need to taste my lover's sex
at least once more before I drown.

We should all reenter the slickness
from which we were torn, the blood-soaked
light that ushers us into a body that lasts
such a brief time.

Night's tissue disassembles beneath the line
of the approaching fires we've drawn.

Burning grouse fly ahead of the blaze, illuminate
a path like sparks from an opened furnace door.

It takes the loon so much effort to be skyborne.
Where she took flight, the water churns with small fish,
and heron gullet the slapping bodies until they turn to statues.

This morning, at the confluence of two tributaries,
I washed up on a sandbar and searched for the rookery.

Begging for one more raven prophecy, coyote tracks
ran me in circles, and I lost any sense of direction.

Trees possess the longest memory. They know each of us
who has slept, or eaten, or wept beneath them.

I held the moon last night, pushed my arm into a crater
and brought forth the skeleton of the first bear
who watched over earth's making.

Bodies in May

I ate for two moons
since rising with
the rising rivers
in the greening
days when trees
flower and grubs
wriggle beneath
rotting logs when
the earth warmed
and I slept without
hunger and found
more than enough
to eat in my walking
that is why
I was surprised
by the painful
emptiness I felt
after she gave
herself and I
entered the door
of her body
and left something
of myself
to grow apart
from me.

A Map

On pain of death, scratch pictures
in the dust.
—ELEANOR ROSS TAYLOR

He couldn't be sure where he was. It had been dark
when he started. He remembered the smell of winterberry
crushed but didn't know the word to name it. An animal moved
in the underbrush. Branches scraped the skin around his eyes,
scratches like tributaries of the river that broke these mountains
at the northern border. The sun rose slowly, like a porcupine
scaling a hemlock. He'd left his parents in hiding. It was unclear
when they'd crossed the invisible boundary illegally. At the end
of each day, he tried to draw a map in the dust to show himself
where he'd passed. Thirst whispered in his ear, told him to listen
for water washing against stone. At a spring he drank to forget
the ache in his throat, to dull his hunger so he might think.

He read the signs left by those before him, and still fear trailed
like a surveyor's chalk-line. On the third night he could no longer
will himself awake. They found him asleep on his belly, bound
his wrists behind his back in rings of plastic, roped him to a four-
wheeler where he was forced to walk or be dragged behind it.
They questioned him in a room made of concrete, lit with a ceiling-
bulb whose wires wound through walls and out into a world
where coal burned and became electricity so the darkness
would never descend and no one could move without their knowing.
When they asked where he came from, he didn't speak, only lifted
his shirt so they might see what he'd done. In those first days,
as he walked away from his parents, each night after drawing
a map in the dirt, he'd take a sharp rock or stick, puncture
his skin, copying the path that would show him a way through,
reminding him, like prayer, where his parents were, knowing
it was safer there than in the valley, how the only thing caught
this high on the mountain was the wind.

What the Market Will Bear

The moon rises on a string attached to the earth: a girl who only remembers her mother when the sun shines and pulls at the tether. In that kind of light, we stack slabs of meat on ice, having baited the deer with salt, halted them with a spotlight from the truck. The rattle of boxcar doors as the train pulls away sounds like the turning of a lock. Flesh fails, whether arrested or not, and anything we mount mills in dust remade as desert. In the suburbs, where this meat is headed, they still sprinkle their lawns, teenage boys shedding shirts to mow and groom the shrubs. Drones replace the shadows of birds, peering into windows for information that's not theirs. Like groundhogs, we bed down in holes, coal-swollen tongues having ruined the taste of meat. Whatever sprouts, we eat.

Pawpaw Elegy

Ointment for a troubled dream, feast to fill an ache, and so the bear
crooks a small tree to the earth, arm bent like a shepherd's hook, feet
treading branches, improvised hay rake to comb the oblong fruits

into tall grasses that grow along the oxbowed river. A boy will learn
that a stream, as it ages, changes direction as it pleases, drowning those
we love in spring floods. The fruit smashes, yellow custard squeezed

between leaves, a skin Ursus licks and teethes, wresting pleasure
from the sunlight trapped within. The boy watches from beneath
a cluster of witch hazel. His father, at dinner each night, said,

The feast is everywhere! But since his death, the food on the plate
congeals like a limp tongue, unable to taste anything but grief.
Everything the bear eats builds along its rump, shaped into fat,

weaving a blanket of flesh before there's nothing left and winter
drapes him in sleep. The pawpaw's bean-shaped seeds slide
down the gullet, and the squeaky wheel of a goldfinch call

falls and begs joy from air. The boy's mother has asked him to pick
the fruit for the pudding she'll curd, the loaf she'll bake, adding
spiceberries and black walnuts to brighten the taste. The oven smells

like memory. In woods he's known since birth, he turns blankly
and wonders where home is, stares at tree trunks and repeats
their names as his father taught him. Still the shovel scrapes

sour mud from the coffin, and he weeps over the carelessness
of water. On the river path the bear acts as farmer: seed-filled
turds crushed and oozing with muck, newly planted orchard

to feed fox and woodchuck. In the boy's palm, the darkened green
of a pawpaw wobbles. His father would have cut a cross
with his Barlow knife to test the color. He tears a patch

of the fruit's roughened skin, wiggles fingers in the breadbasket,
bringing the doughy center to lips, a father's kiss, a groan
of grieving delight.

Ursus Considers the First Gospel of Snake

When the hermit thrush disappears from the branch,
Ursus blows and clacks his teeth, trying to bring back
the brown bird by borrowing its song. He thinks
about the insides of things and kills a vireo, opening
its flank with a nail. He's disappointed no music rushes out.
With moonlight's help, on the road near the river,
he finds a mink, and where a tire separated the flesh
picks at the crushed stomach and spleen. He wonders
what he would look like turned inside out and wishes
he could unhinge his jaw like the snake he saw devour
a bullfrog. He'd take into his mouth all those who walk
or wiggle or crawl this road, guide them to the back
of his throat, then settle them safe in the belly's cave.

The Cedars in the Pasture

I.

In afternoon shadow, the sharp smell of cedar opens
as the girl walks the far pasture, unmown in more
than a decade. Fallow and left to become fertile, young
cedars have begun to take back the land, feeding waxwings
who fly through their limbs and grow drunk on the tree's
blue fruit, a soft glow fermenting beneath their skins.

II.

Before we're born we all live in water. The ancient forests
the first people knew, who bore all life, were felled by the girl's
ancestors when they sailed across the ocean in ships built of cedar,
thinking God bestowed all things upon them. They didn't believe
the stories of spirits who lived beneath bark, who spoke in spring
storms when cedar fronds quaked, or how humans, as they rot
back into the world that made them, become grass
and goldenrod, a sapling looking up at an infinite sky.

III.

The girl only knows the scars of recent history:
Fifty years since the last of the coal was stripped,
traveling back in time, layer by layer, descending
a shaft to bring darkness to the surface. And now:
without any shame, we construct machines
that make a mountain disappear, no regard
for the memory or souls of trees.

IV.

In the gloaming, before night reaches the cedars
in the pasture, in May's new warmth when her father
plows the fields, the smell of copper curves
along her grandmother's spine, and the old woman
takes a crow's feather from a chest made of cedar.
Like an aging river, she tells the girl how cedars share
their long lives, joining us to water and sky, providing
passage through the body of this unnamed country.

V.

Especially on the hottest days, the girl has trouble catching
her breath, drowning in a sky of cotton. When the dust in the hayloft
fogs the air, and the chemicals her father sprays on the fields linger,
or in the rain of dried leaves the combine sends toward heaven
in September, the world, as we've remade it, settles in her chest,
and her mother brings an inhaler to her mouth.

VI.

Each year the girl raises a cow to sell at the county fair, throws hay
down the chute, carries water to the trough. In the heat of the day
she opens the gate. The cow wanders a worn path to the river
to soak. After her chores, she follows the tracks, coming over
a knoll to see a cedar shaking as the cow's hind quarters
rub and bend the branches like a stiff comb.

VII.

In the floodplain, hidden by a drapery of willow shoots,
sits a giant cedar stump. Afternoons the girl and a friend
make a nest in the decaying center, circling their bodies
to follow the coil of the tree's past life. Only a portion
of the sky can be seen, and they pretend their clothes are green
flowers, skin the gold of aspen leaves in October. They eat
wild strawberries at the beginning of June, lips red with sugar.
The air fills with the fragrance of honeysuckle, and the girl
stands to sing, *Let everything that blossoms blossom!*

VIII.

The pasture is mottled by the shadows of clouds passing. The cedars,
erect and alert, look like a children's choir practicing: chins jut and mouths
chant the words of a song that calls for light to come, for soil to offer
what it can, for rain to fall when it might. The girl begins to sing, too,
but instead of folding her hands in prayer, she strokes the cedar's fern-like
fingers, remembering her mother's hands rubbing her back, her father's
goodnight kiss on her cheek, hallway light a sliver on the floor,
and the sound of the trees growing in the dark as she sleeps, bones
stretching, each waking four inches taller.

For Aimee Nezhukumatathil

Ursus Grows Wings

Ursus's body commands he eat,
to rake bushels of apples
from orchard trees and gorge
upon the night-dark sweetness
of the last blackberry. He craves
the sharp lemon of sorrel, acorn
meal upon the tongue, breath ripe
with the smashed ferment
of hawthorn.

Ursus climbs an ancient tulip
poplar that rots from the inside out.
Near the peak a hole to crawl through,
to slide down into a pit, a sacristy
where he can sleep and dream
of what he came into this world
knowing. Ursus can't explain,
but his heart feels like a boat
about to capsize, sailors
tumbling over the bow, some
drowning in the surf.

In his torpor Ursus struggles
to find the stars that signify him.
The animal of his throat aches
for a prayer that might hold
back the seconds, sky collapsing
into darkness.

Where constellations swim
Ursus assumes a dead man's float,
exhales a final breath, and sinks
beneath the amniotic tide. As he sleeps
he feels a sharp stab at the shoulder:
vision of wings sprouting—axillars,
patagium, coverts of the upper wing
and tail—all springing from air.

And tracked through, struts
and trusses, the scaffolding for flight,
because he may be at sea for years,
like those pelagic birds that glide
over shore, never coming to rest
on land.

He can't be sure if the dark
has receded, snail drawing its head
into a spiraled shell. It's the whine
of a saw that wakes him. Smell
of burning oil like feathers in flame.

Ursus scrambles upward
from a raven's dream and leaps
from the hole before the poplar
can fall. In his flying he looks down
at a man who cuts a final notch,
steering this tree to earth.
The man jerks head up
toward branch-crash
and watches Ursus, arms
spread, slide down the trunk
of a neighboring oak.

Claws can write history, but
it's the ursine body loping
unsteadily into a grove of beech
that presses the human mind:
those last leaves to go, copper-
gold, like the light that shines
around the heads of saints, vestigial
wings flapping at their backs.

Learning to Tie a Fly

Under an April sun, the sister spies a speckled trout
fanning along the flat stones in the creekbed that divides

the mountain. Like these fish, her brother hides
in a fold formed when an ancient sea retreated,

leaving strewn rocks where flies hatch, emerging
from casings on the bottom. She hollers his name,

and he appears from between a crevice.
Together they wade a pool that drops beneath

a small waterfall, a swirling place they've been told
not to go. Insects crowd the air with translucent wings,

which the boy describes for his sister, telling her
how their father spins and turns them at a workbench

in the basement: crafting thoraxes, claspers,
and twin tails, the colors that cause fish to rise

like parentheses, to gorge with a greed that hardens
their bellies. The girl loves when her mother cooks

the backstrap from the deer her father kills,
and she believes the animal resides inside her body,

helping her to run, to trace paths through the forest.
When her brother slips, tripping on a stone and sliding

beneath the foam, she shouts and dives, plunging
under the water where she sees nothing

except white bubbles of oxygen, the red and blue
dots along the sides of fish as they scatter

to hide among the rocks. For more than a week
there's only emptiness, and finally a rescue diver

surfaces with the body more than a mile downriver.
Partway through summer, with her parents

she scatters her brother's ashes in the stream,
trout gulping little pieces of bone. The girl imagines

how he's become the river, swimming in a different body,
finding new places to hide. By August her father loses

his job at the foundry, and her mother sleeps most of the day.
The girl says nothing and disappears into her room

where she's stolen her father's tying tools,
along with bits of deer hide and feathers from birds

fallen to earth. In an old book, she reads the name
deer caddis like an incantation and follows the instructions.

With a barbed hook in the vice jaws and thread
from her mother's sewing basket, she binds the hair,

attaches plumage to sculpt the hackle, fashioning
with tenderness a lie to float across a riffle. Each day

she ties another, examining the photo in the book,
picturing how it will look to a fish finning in the current.

With the leaves turning, she climbs the mountain
to that swirling place, casts the fly she's made,

and from the depths brilliant colors bend
the rod into a question mark. The strength

of the fish, the surge back toward where it came from,
what it was before it was a trout: muscle shaking

like when she held her brother, tickling him
until laughter cascaded from his mouth.

Lost Blue

For more than
a decade I stole
snowmelt
from spring,
lifted pink
and red bodies
twisting
from current,
the only fish
born rightfully
to this place.
But after
the fire ran up
the mountain—
(root balls
incinerated,
a scorched
absence large
enough to crawl
inside of)—
the stream holds
only ash,
water warmed
without banked
dogwood and willow,
the leaky canoes
of fir and spruce
sunk to the bottom.
I count every fish
as it swims away
to the main river:
orphans of the lost
blue I'd hoped

to show my son
before the debt
of loving a place
broke him.

dream elevator

After the man rapes the boy

      he climbs the cellar stairs

and walks

      into the woods

    that border the farm's farthest field.

He smells himself and considers

              how sin stains the sinner.

The boy cries in a corner

    of the cellar, remembering

      three crows

who drank from the pond.

           Blood smears his jeans,

    and he crawls

up the steps,

      goes to the bureau in the bedroom

where the key

to the gun safe is kept.

The man stands creek side,

trousers circled

at his feet. Sun clangs on water

as he washes his cock,

balls shriveled in the April cold.

Exposed and weak,

like the stalk of a fern,

the boy lifts the shotgun

from the rack. His shoulders shake

as he sights the barrel.

His father taught him to exhale

before pulling the trigger.

This past November he shot a deer

and steam rose from the gut pile:

lungs and intestines like an altar.

The sound of water pushing

against stone

masks the bear's approach.

The animal has also smelled the sin

and followed his hunger.

The man grasps his own scrotum

and thinks how he could cut away

this part of himself,

leave it to drown in the stream.

He's watched

the boy at mass

as he carries the thurible, ashamed

that he's aroused

by the scent of incense.

Before he can decide

the bear rides the man's head

down against the rocks,

clawing open the chest,

breaking four ribs

and tearing them

from the sternum.

Halfway across the field

the boy hears a scream

and runs.

What he sees is a body

that looks like a broken

vase.

Purple and white

flowers cling to the rim

of the wound,

and the slick petals

of that damnable

heart

rankle

as Ursus chews

the right ventricle.

This Tired Flesh

Emerald ash borer killed the trees on the mountain. The government cut the ones closest to the road and burned the wood before we could gather it. A half-day's walk into the forest there's a clearing where hundreds of rotting chestnut stumps rise like an upside-down graveyard of dinosaur heads. A meth lab in an old hunting trailer blew up last winter, sending smoke signals skyward and two cousins life-flighted to the burn unit in Pittsburgh. When a coyote crossed my path, it lowered its tail and didn't look back at me. They kill the very young and the very old. To eat an elder you have to allow for scar tissue, which takes the longest to chew. The kingfisher that divebombs the creek reminds me we live in a world of flight. The girl who lifted my heart off the ground was fed rattlesnake in the crib. Friday night she put a drop of acid on my tongue, and for the past three days I've hung on the point of a waning moon, peering down at her breasts through a threadbare dress. Her grandmother fried everything in bacon grease until her heart stopped while smoking a pipe on the back porch. After we put the old woman in the ground, the girl's meth-head brothers scoured the mountain for dens, pouring diesel down holes. When they dropped the struck match, purple and orange flames thrashed the air for hours. Some of the snakes slithered out, scales on fire. The brothers used an ax to cut the heads off, a knife to collect the rattles. The girl I love wears a necklace that shakes when she walks.

Snow's Memory

Come, see real
flowers
of this painful world.
—BASHO

Fires spring up in intolerable heat while air tankers
pick-pocket the reservoir for rain. For the past three

summers July flamed and burned until the end of October.
Most mountains have nothing left to blister. Hair curls

and air shimmers in waves like a shook sheet.
What little water trickles down swims up from springs

fifty feet beneath the scorched surface. Ursus plods,
small ash-clouds rising from the dust of cremated bones:

trees who couldn't run; deer and fox who,
despite a final sprint, flickered out.

Bear possess no sweat glands, and Ursus pants
like a golden retriever, fur singed from a flaring pine.

The water gap remains green in drought, as rhododendron
send straw-roots into the same cup the creek sips.

White and pink flowers appear above leaves
where Ursus slips and rubs a branch maze.

With back petaled like a silk robe, he splashes
scalded feet in the streambed where a fallen tulip tree

serves as a dam, digging a pool three-feet deep.
The bear plunges belly-first, dunks head,

then rolls, as if water were his true bed:
floating, drunk on blue sky, speckled flowers

the color of snow's memory.

Learning to Walk Upright

How I fell into this life of living off others, of being a social
parasite, is a long, sordid story. . . .
—CHARLES JOHNSON

Some thought to become upright citizens meant to stand and walk toward snowcapped mountains where their idea of God thundered for devotion. Ursus can walk upright if he wants but usually chooses not to. He remains unconvinced it leads to any good. In the muddy shallows of his dreams, piscine gills flare as pink lungs suffer an exile from the warm salt of birth. What about the stories of those who climbed the tallest trees, living for a time in concert with their needs? Ursus sees fickleness in pine stumps that rot, trees felled to build ships with empty cargo holds. White men stole black bodies to chain below deck, the only light seeping in where chinking failed. Unlike them, Ursus learned to share the one soul the world gives freely. Before he wakes—sleep failing like a tern with a broken wing—Ursus watches others paddle where the sun licks the sea. Off the starboard bow forgotten cousins fin through indigo waves. At the bottom of the deepest trough an almost human shadow rows toward a spit of sand, shore's frayed edge come undone.

Until Darkness Comes

A 100-year-old gray and ductile iron foundry in Somerset, PA, has issued a closing notice to workers, according to local reports.

The white blades turn the sky: red-
eyed turbines blinking away the danger
of flying things. Small children float up
over the Alleghenies, parents chasing
the dangling ropes of weather balloons.
It's hard to predict when a storm may blow through.
A boy huddles by a bedroom window, wonders
if his father knows where every deer hides
on the mountain. It's his job to pull the sled
when his father makes a kill. He's been taught
in school the wind that circles the blades carries
electricity to the towns where steel was made.

Three years ago his sister disappeared in the clouds,
heat lightning like veins in the sky. She sends a letter
once a month with a weather report and money
their mother uses for an inhaler. Most of the coal dust
has settled, but fires burn on the drilling platforms
and the prehistoric gas smells like the eggs that spoil
in the hutch when the hens hide them.
The boy never wants to leave this place.
Everything important is buried here: his grandparents,
a pocket knife he stole from his best friend, the eye-teeth
of an elk he found poached at the bottom of a ravine.
Yesterday in the barn a carpenter ant drilled a hole.
The boy bent to the sawed-circle and blew into it,
breath forced down into darkness. He dreams each night
of a horse galloping from a barn, mane on fire
like a shooting star. He prays for a coat sewn from pigeon
feathers, for small wings to fly over the tops of trees
where the children land when their balloons begin to wilt.

On summer evenings barn swallows careen like drones,
gorging dragonflies that skim the swamp.
The birds' blue shoulders cant and angle, breast
the color of the foundry's smokestacks as they crumble
beneath wrecking balls and bulldozers, extinguishing
the mill fires the boy's grandfather never dreamt
would go out.

Of This World

A warbler beats its wings at the blueness,
and a brown boy raises an arm in praise.

Somewhere the tongue of God laps water
where the wind crosses the surface.

On the logging road a ruffed grouse drums,
and the bodies of the dead ripen with stories.

The true passage of time is marked
by what birds and trees perceive.

Too often I sought to kiss grief's lips
when I was young.

Now I'm old, it's no pleasure to watch
the chickadee peck a winterkilled deer.

A dove flies down from the moon,
and a woman lifts a baby to a breast.

On the mountain a bear eats two berries, imprisoning
the honeyed darkness on the tongue's underside.

How did I ever forget all the world's
an upper room?

For Bryce, Brandon, and Brock Macon

Watershed

When you go deep, following a winding river to its source,
you're soon bewildered, wandering a place beyond knowing.
—HSIEH LING-YÜN

Questions between branches roost in hemlocks along the stream.

Growing upward into the skull, the orange ghost of porcupine teeth
scores the tree's cartilage.

Answers unravel in creases, like the yellow yarn of witch-hazel flowers:
folds folding over into narrowing passes.

This is the only way through.

A hundred thousand years ago the currents of an inland sea erected a
sandstone altar.

If you look at the winding gap, the striations become clear.

As Ursus climbs higher, the stream winnows, speaking the names of the dead.

On the other side of the mountain, water flows in the opposite direction.

Winter Solstice

I listen to dried goldenrod, an oak gall
swaying on a branch. These gray moments

test patience. At the edge of the field
a deer steps over a fallen maple.

The winged seeds of hornbeam rattle,
so much like the sound of an antler

scraping bark, fashioning a bit of light
where there was none.

When I Survey the Wondrous Cross

Could we do this on purpose, deliberately producing artificial
clouds to reduce global warming?
—BBC

We stole the panels
that collected light.
Unbolted them
from roof tops,
gathered them in
from the pastures
where they'd grazed
on the sun
like sheep.

Their tiled faces
tilted
toward the god
who powered
our homes, our cars,
the screens
we watched
with devotion.

Who doesn't seek
after illumination?
With the sky
covered
in darkness,
there was no point
anymore.

We built the main
beam out of truck
beds and trash
dumpsters,
the arms
from car doors.
We towed
boxcars
from the railyard
to serve
as the foot.

We kept fires
burning; more coal
than it was worth.

As we scored
and latched
the metal,
attaching
the shiny boards,
I didn't know
whether
I believed.

It grew taller,
higher
than the water
tower
at the end
of Main Street,
more than two
thousand
panels
before it was
complete.

We assembled
at dawn,
although
it had been
months
since we'd seen
the sun.

We lifted
our arms,
begged
the clouds
to divide.

We chanted
and prayed,
called its name
in as many
languages
as we knew.

Then we sang
the old hymn.
Our grandmothers
starting each
verse,
teaching us
our part.

Museum: Ursus americanus

They took our bodies.
Dismembered some.
Displayed paws,
claws, eyes outside
of sockets. Others
they stuffed
and stood on wired
legs. A caricature
of the way we rise
when seeking
the source
of some noise
or clawing a beech
to tell another
about the place
they're entering.
Worse were
the skinned ones.
Bodies suspended
on hooks, pink
muscle exposed.
When we're stripped
of our fur, we look
so much like the ones
who did this.

How to Measure Sea Level Rise

In the crowns of the last white pines, children climb
broad limbs, an escape ladder with a clean view to the horizon.
Like the calving of glaciers, you can hear from a long way off

where the land closest to the water folds and buckles.
Because this brackish estuary poisons roots, we collect rainwater
from leaves and after storms cast nets, hoping for the rare mackerel,

an eel or squid to swim into the knots of our vacant stomachs.
A different warmth engulfs this raft of branches, and winds
from the south rock the dying trees. Some of us are lulled to sleep,

bodies slipping from their perches to plunge toward earth.
The drowned catch on skeletons of coral reefs and wave
like bloated flags in surrender. The moon rides the wrack line,

then disappears. We huddle together in the dark, water lapping
at ankles, asking into what harbor we might sail, where any of us
might safely drop anchor.

When the Stones Are Undone

Their faces will be like flames.
—ISAIAH 13:8

We sang "Shall We Gather at the River," and the preacher cried out
that only God knows when the stones of the temple will fall.
After the sixth hurricane made landfall, the dam failed like a broken cage,
and the reservoir washed down the mountain. Water possesses the longest
memory. When freed it carves a path that may last ten thousand years.
In disbelief we wave our hands through empty air: stone replaced
by a language long-forgotten, spoken in words a river invents
as it topples trees, houses, barns, as it carries cars a mile downstream.
More than fifty years since the Cuyahoga River caught fire, factory waste
a flammable icing. Now gas leaks from the submerged station
and a spark flares. With each explosion, in the firelit dark we smear ash
on foreheads and breasts, croak cries similar to the burning herons
and egrets, who stumble on air, no longer able to fly above the flames
of God's unguarded jaws.

In the Garden

When the last pollinator fluttered its wings and folded
into itself, like newspaper as it catches flame,
we'd already buried the skeletons of the remaining
hummingbirds, the husks of bees, what little was left
of the antennae of moths and butterflies, the tiny corpses
of the penultimate wasp and ant, the sting and bite
of these small lives no longer a threat. Nothing had to be done
for the scurrying beetles who burrowed into caskets
of their own making, but some of us hung the now still
bodies of swerving bats from lampposts, while others gathered
them in nets, making pilgrimages to caves to lay them to rest.
At a museum in Washington, DC, small brass plates named
each creature, explained their place in the vanishing taxonomy.
Underground installations housed seeds for plants and trees,
and we collected an example of each species
that played a role in fertilization, pinned them to a board
with elaborate charts that identified body parts
and their peculiar uses. We were most interested in
their mechanical efficiency and wished to recover
the ways they conveyed pollen from anther to stigma.
We brought in theologians who revised the sign of the cross,
a version that emphasized reproductive organs
and the importance of fecundity. Even the scientists believed
resurrection, grown in a Petri dish, was our only chance:
stigmata marking the wings of a swallowtail or monarch,
each of us longing to touch the holes we'd help to make
in the colorful fabric. This was our prayer to unburden us
of doubt, and despite our lack of faith, we ached for a peach
at the end of a branch, a plum or apple, the honeyed pears
we greedily ate in August, juice dribbling from our chins,
fingers sticky with our own undoing. The few scientists
who were not already living off-planet began to create
new designs for our children's hands and lips,

working to enhance the ridges in the brain that help
to discern and process olfactory signals. They wrote code
while the future slept in its fleshly rooms, reprogramming
the cells for stunted growth, perfectly proportioned
for the work that lay ahead. Where some might have seen
deformity, we saw beauty: sons and daughters walking
orchard rows, crawling between cornstalks and vineyard grapes,
scaling almond trees whose cupped blossoms waited to be filled
with our answers. The children stopped at each bloom,
stooped with fingers shaped like paintbrushes, caressing
silky petals as grains of pollen caught against their skin,
enough static so this precious dusting wouldn't fall away,
until they delivered it to a flower of our choosing.

To Wake from Long Sleep in Darkness

> *Explosions of grief,*
> *Diving into the sea of death,*
> *Like the stars of the wheeling Bear.*
> —ROBERT BLY

Along the coast darkened cities
crumble while Venus shines
brightly above Jupiter.

Like the phosphorescent glow
of jellyfish, Ursus sways
through meteor showers.

Sinking into light's reflection,
he dreams of women who are half-fox,
half-otter, of children who are more fawn
than human.

Ursus never dreams of men as other
than the thing they are.

Constellations swim, and he struggles
against the tide to find the star
that will guide him.

The ends of green branches float.
He reaches out to touch
roosting birds, gentle caress
along the feathers of the back.

Despite the disappearance
of artic terns, armies and navies
follow their own shadows north.

A river of milky light oxbows
Ursus's eyes. Farther away
the hum of a greater light
on the far edge of the horizon.

What Ursus believes is the morning star
is actually a flash of sun on the metal
wings of a plane.

When the sky falls to the ground,
Ursus yearns for a starry crown
to rest upon his head.

What We Died For

Things great and strong dwell below.
Things soft and weak dwell above.
—LAO TZU

Like the summer fires that blackened the mountain,
a virus spread, burrowing into the dead carcasses

of bear and deer. Crows picked at the tainted meat
and flew with the disease to the valley. With each death,

before the bodies stiffened into planks, we kneaded
forearms and calves, pressed thumbs into corded

back muscles, bending legs so knees touched chest.
In April, when the soot-covered earth softened,

we dug round holes to fit seed-corpses to the crumbling edges.
We prayed as we took turns with the shovel, a liturgy

of vanishing names in the book of lost species:
elm and chestnut and ash. Now in the charred air,

we ask those who remain to return to the burial ground,
to make note in the ledger if any tree sprouts

from the bodies we planted.

Sitting Shiva

If you find the bones of a bear, sit down and stay with them.
The dead desire our company. Touch each one—scapula,
tibia, ulna—even the tiniest bones of the hind and forefeet,
the curve of every claw. Just out of sight, a thrush will sing.
Bird song is a way to speak in secret. Find comfort
in the arbutus that whitens each March on the old logging road.
Wait until dark. A full moon will rise from the bear's skull,
showing what she thought of us. Hold the moon-skull in your lap,

stroke the cranial ridges. You may see your dead father
scaling the talus to the blueberry field where this bear ate,
mouth sated and purpled by the sweetest fruit. Your mother
will be in the room on the second floor of the house, packing
and then unpacking a box of your father's clothes. It's hard
to give up this life. But we must. Others are waiting behind us.

Acknowledgments

My thanks to the editors of the following journals or publications in which these poems first appeared, sometimes in different form.

About Place Journal: "dream elevator" (2) and "dream elevator" (3)
Appalachia: "Bog Parable" and "The Book of Miracles"
Arts & Letters: "Learning to Tie a Fly"
Atlanta Review: "Snow's Memory"
basalt: "dream elevator" (4) and "Foxfire"
Blueline: "Winter Solstice"
Chautauqua: "A Map," "Dowser," "Foot Washing," and "Ursus Grows Wings"
Cold Mountain Review: "Of This World" and "When the Stones Are Undone"
descant: "Extinction" and "Music for Film before the Destruction of a Drone"
The Fourth River: "Bad Seed" and "Snapper"
The Gettysburg Review: "Buck Day"
Hampden-Sydney Poetry Review: "Coffin Honey"
The Hollins Critic: "What Her Father Taught Her"
The Hopper: "Pawpaw Elegy"
Image: "Relics"
Iron Horse Literary Review: "If We Have to Go"
The Learned Pig (United Kingdom): "Lambing" and "Museum: *Ursus americanus*"
The Midnight Oil: "Lost Blue"
The Missouri Review: "Mother" and "Taxidermy: *Cathartes aura*"
Natural Bridge: "As the Mountain Grows Dark"
North American Review: "What I Know about the Last Lynching in Jeff Davis County"
Orion: "Sitting Shiva"
Permafrost: "Watershed"
Phoebe: "This Tired Flesh"
Poet Lore: "Bear-Eater" and "The Cedars in the Pasture"
Poetry East: "Churching the Cow"
Poetry Northwest: "Until Darkness Comes"
The South Carolina Review: "What We Died For"
Talking River Review: "Hunting with Dogs," "Learning to Walk Upright," and "To Wake from Long Sleep in Darkness"
Tar River Poetry: "Rooster"
Terrain.org: "In the Garden"
Under a Warm Green Linden: "Bodies in May" and "How to Measure Sea Level Rise"
Western Humanities Review: "Field Sermon" and "Ursus in the Underworld"
Willow Springs: "Possum"

Maggie Smith selected "What I Know about the Last Lynching in Jeff Davis County" as runner-up for the 2021 James Hearst Poetry Prize from the *North American Review*.

"A Map" was nominated for a Pushcart Prize by *Chautauqua*.

"As the Mountain Grows Dark" was nominated for a Pushcart Prize by *Natural Bridge*.

"This Tired Flesh" was a finalist for the Greg Grummer Prize from *Phoebe*.

"What We Died For" was reprinted by Verse Daily.

"In the Garden" was reprinted in *Dear America: Letters of Hope, Habitat, Defiance, and Democracy*, ed. Derek Sheffield, Simmons Buntin, and Elizabeth Dodd (San Antonio: Trinity University Press, 2020).

"Until Darkness Comes" was reprinted in *Rewilding: Poems for the Environment*, ed. Crystal S. Gibbins (Minneapolis: Flexible Press, 2020).

"The Cedars in the Pasture" was published by Field Works as part of a limited-edition LP, CD, and Risograph comic book, *Cedars*, with illustrations by Maria Medem and music arranged and produced by Stuart Hyatt.

"Taxidermy: *Cathartes aura*" also appeared in *Native Species* (East Lansing: Michigan State University Press, 2019).

All translations of the quoted lines from Lao Tzu, Wei Ying-wu, Wang Wei, and Hsieh Ling-Yün are by David Hinton.

The translation of the quoted lines from Basho are by Lucien Stryk.

Thanks to the following people for their continued encouragement as I make my poems: Jan Beatty, Lori Bechtel-Wherry, Tanya and Wendell Berry, Brian Black, Craig Blietz, Dave Bonta, Taylor Brorby, Lauren Camp, Catherine Cocks, James Crews, Jim Daniels, Geffrey Davis, Joyce Davis, Nathan Davis, Shelly Davis, Alison Hawthorne Deming, Chris Dombrowski, David James Duncan, Camille Dungy, Don Flenar, Don and Punky Fox, Michael Garrigan, Ross Gay, Dan Gerber, Andy Gottlieb, Leah Naomi Green, Jeff Gundy, Parkman Howe, Henry Hughes, Elise Jajuga, Jonathan Johnson, Virginia Kasamis, Julia Spicher Kasdorf, Helen Kiklevich, Ted Kooser, Daniel Lassell, Chris La Tray, Don and Melinda Lanham, Carolyn Mahan, Adrian Matejka, Shara McCallum, Doug Miller, Dinty Moore, Erin Murphy, Aimee Nezhukumatathil, Ron Rash, Mary Rose O'Reilley, Sean Prentiss, Scott Russell Sanders, Derek Sheffield, Jack Ridl, Pattiann Rogers, Melanie Viets, Patricia Jabbeh Wesley, Ken Womack, and Dana Young.

A special thanks to four wonderful writers who read this book in various stages and helped to make it better: Noah Davis, Katie Hays, Lee Peterson, and Steve Sherrill.

And to Dave Shumate, who reads my poems weekly, at times daily, a conversation we've carried on in poems for many years, gratitude and appreciation. I'm so deeply thankful for our friendship and the ways you understand me through your kind and attentive care with my most unpolished and raw work.

Many of these poems were finished with the assistance of generous grants from the Pennsylvania State University.

Todd Davis is the author of seven full-length collections of poetry—*Coffin Honey*, *Native Species*, *Winterkill*, *In the Kingdom of the Ditch*, *The Least of These*, *Some Heaven*, and *Ripe*—as well as of a limited-edition chapbook, *Household of Water, Moon, and Snow*. He edited the nonfiction collection, *Fast Break to Line Break: Poets on the Art of Basketball*, and coedited the anthology *Making Poems*. His writing has won the Midwest Book Award, the Gwendolyn Brooks Poetry Prize, the *Chautauqua* Editors Prize, the Bloomsburg University Book Prize, and the Foreword INDIES Book of the Year Silver and Bronze Awards. His poems appear in such noted journals and magazines as *American Poetry Review*, *Alaska Quarterly Review*, *Barrow Street*, *Iowa Review*, *North American Review*, *Missouri Review*, *Gettysburg Review*, *Orion*, *Poetry Northwest*, *Western Humanities Review*, *Willow Springs*, *Sycamore Review*, Verse Daily, and Poetry Daily. He teaches environmental studies, creative writing, and American literature at Pennsylvania State University's Altoona College.